Encountering Christ

Conversations with Women in John's Gospel

Magdalen Lawler SND

A Redemptorist Publication

Published by Redemptorist Publications

Copyright © Redemptorist Publications
A Registered Charity limited by guarantee.

Text by Sister Magdalen Lawler SND
Design: Rosemarie Pink

Cover image from an Icon of the Woman at the Well, presented to the late
Fr Joseph Gill SJ in recognition of his work of dialogue with Orthodox Christians.
Icon reproduced by kind permission of the Jesuit Community, Manresa House,
Birmingham, England.

First published by Redemptorist Publications as *Intimate Moments* January 1995
New edition as *Encountering Christ* published January 2005

Scripture texts are taken from the New Jerusalem Bible, published and copyright
1985 by Darton, Longman and Todd Ltd and Doubleday & Co Inc, and used by
permission of the publishers.

ISBN 0 85231 296 2

Printed in Britain by: CKN Print Ltd., Northampton, NN3 8RQ

Redemptorist
PUBLICATIONS

Alphonsus House Chawton Alton Hampshire GU34 3HQ
Telephone 01420 88222   Fax 01420 88805
rp@ShineOnline.net   www.ShineOnline.net

CONTENTS

Preface

In baptism we are all called to full discipleship which implies intimacy with Jesus; as experienced and revealed by the mother of Jesus and so many of his women-followers.

These women can lead us through a way of prayer, which requires a small amount of quiet each day. Ten or fifteen minutes would be a good way to start. It can be very helpful to look for natural "oases of quiet" in your day – for instance, in the bath, walking the dog, turning off the radio on a car journey, cooking or washing, or pottering in the garden or with your tool-box. When you have learnt to recognise the quiet moment, clear a space and begin to savour it. Make it intentional, so that the shortest time can be a clear space into which God can enter without constraint.

This is a book that is meant to be prayed through rather than read and laid aside. In fact, only a small amount of time is sometimes needed for prayer in a busy life. There are many instances in scripture where we are reminded that God's work continues in us whether we are asleep or awake. That can be a great consolation for those of us who immediately doze off when we begin to pray. For many parents the only quiet time they have is just before they fall asleep. However, it is better to begin to pray with a couple of minutes at your disposal than not to begin because you are waiting for the time when you will have a full hour, or an afternoon, or a weekend, or whatever you think is the perfect scenario.

Each encounter has suggestions for how you can enter into the scene and become familiar with the very fabric of the life of Jesus. Try to use your imagination in order to do this. All your senses are called into play to help you to enter into the scene, but, more importantly, to help you to recognise your own feelings and moods in praying the event, so that it becomes easier to spot its relevance in your present situation and the action of God in the "here and now" of your own life.

Praying with the Imagination

PRAYING WITH ALL OF OURSELVES

This book is about praying with all of our senses to help us to have a real encounter with Jesus. It uses the stories involving women in the Gospel of John. Many women in the Fourth Gospel are portrayed in a very positive way, and in intimate relationship with Jesus. No woman is ever shown as resisting Jesus' revelation or as failing to believe in him. Yet they all appear as striking individuals.

Many of these encounters are characterised by a dialogue, a real conversation in which Jesus is guiding that person through an experience which will lead her to a far deeper knowledge and appreciation of his significance in her life. Jesus met each woman exactly where she was and touched her in a very special way. Through their stories, Jesus can touch us in our own lives, whether men or women, and we, too, can talk with him and come to a deeper understanding of him.

Beginning with Mary, his mother, we shall read their personal stories and try to remember Jesus as he invited us to do.

SENSES ARE A MEMORY BANK

Most of us are blessed with five senses. Some even have a so-called sixth sense which seems to be stronger in some people than in others.

We all enjoy a good meal; we love to look at a fine landscape, or we join in infectious laughter. We delight in the perfume of a flower and we reach out to a little child. However, this is describing those gifts at their most obvious. We all know that at certain times one sense or another may be highly sensitised. We may be more deeply stimulated, for example, in our sense of smell, or touch or taste. This heightened sensitivity may be dependent on our physical or emotional state. So it is difficult to separate the senses from the whole of our function as a person. We also know that a musician or an artist, for example, may not only have a highly developed sense of visual perception or of hearing, but he or she will probably have this gift combined with a lively creativity which is harder to measure. Emotions, too, will come into play, but we can also be sure that much time and effort will have been devoted to developing the gift of sight or hearing and honing it to perfection.

IMAGINATIVE SENSES

Most of us have no doubt about our physical senses, even if their use and function are often "blurred" by other factors. But we have imaginative senses, too: senses that we can exercise in the imagination. For example, we can all imagine lying on a tropical Caribbean beach, even if we have never been there! We can hear the lapping of the waves on the shore and we can feel the grains between our fingers and toes as we lie there in the sand. But the clever part is to notice how we are feeling as we imagine ourselves on this beach. Do you feel good? Comfortable? Refreshed? Or maybe you feel guilty that you should be doing something else?

INTERIOR SENSES

We've thought a bit about our imaginative senses, but these only "make sense" in prayer if we realise that their purpose is to lead us to our interior senses and to make us much more aware of these. For each one of us has a set of corresponding interior senses "of the heart", as it were, and these enable us to come into direct contact with God in different ways. We can see with eyes of the heart, for example, and we hear, too, with inner ears. We have several examples of this in the Gospels: when Mary "pondered all these things in her heart"; when the disciples on the Emmaus road said, "Did not our hearts burn within us when he spoke to us on the road?" In the Hebrew Testament the Psalmist tells us to "Taste and see that the Lord is good!" Using the imaginative senses in prayer is simply an "exercise bike" to get the heart really working, and just as a real exercise bike gets the heart pumping and the blood coursing, so, too, the use of the senses can put us in touch with the real life-centre of our being; the life of God that dwells in our heart. By praying the Gospel of John, we hope to understand more fully the words of the Gospel writer, when he says, "No one has ever seen God; it is the only Son, who is close to the Father's heart who has made him known." Then we discover, too, that we have interior knowledge, as well, so that we just know what being in touch with God feels like because Jesus shows us how the heart of God beats.

In this book you are invited to use your imaginative senses in prayer, in the hope that your heart will be moved and you will come to understand, more fully, the gift of God which surpasses knowledge or understanding. There will be a "widening" of the heart and mind to embrace people and concepts hitherto unknown or ignored.

Read each Gospel passage as many times as you wish. Read it slowly and stop when something strikes you or when you feel God is speaking to you; when you are ready, set the passage aside and begin to pray with your imagination.

The Wedding Feast at Cana

A Dialogue with the Mother of Jesus

Three days later there was a wedding at Cana in Galilee. The mother of Jesus was there, and Jesus and his disciples had also been invited. When they ran out of wine, since the wine provided for the wedding was all finished, the mother of Jesus said to him, "They have no wine". Jesus said, "Woman, why turn to me? My hour has not come yet." His mother said to the servants, "Do whatever he tells you". There were six stone water jars standing there, meant for the ablutions that are customary among the Jews: each could hold twenty or thirty gallons. Jesus said to the servants, "Fill the jars with water", and they filled them to the brim. "Draw some out now" he told them "and take it to the steward." They did this; the steward tasted the water, and it had turned into wine. Having no idea where it came from – only the servants who had drawn the water

knew – the steward called the bridegroom and said,
"People generally serve the best wine first, and keep
the cheaper sort till the guests have had plenty to drink;
but you have kept the best wine till now". This was the
first of the signs given by Jesus: it was given at Cana
in Galilee. (John 2:1-11)

The first part of John's Gospel is sometimes known as "The Book of Signs". The first sign that Jesus gives us about the deep significance of his relationship with God is his miracle at the wedding party at Cana. This first of his signs is performed at the bidding of a woman, his mother. It has all the characteristics of a dialogue, as we have just noticed.

But have you ever remarked that Mary seems to be the focus for this story? In fact, she is mentioned first in the story. "Jesus and his disciples had also been invited" seems almost an afterthought at first glance, though the friends of the bridegroom would have escorted the bride to the bridegroom's house.

By now, Mary would have been a middle-aged woman. Try to imagine her feelings as she prepares herself for the wedding. What do you think passes through her mind? Do you think she is the bride's relative or perhaps a kinswoman of the bridegroom? Try to see Mary's own wedding preparations or those of the bride.

See and hear the commotion and the joy of the wedding party as it arrives. See the guests milling around. Look at the jewellery of the women, their veils and the colour of their clothes. See the men arrive, too. Hear their voices and sense the jostling of the guests.

Smell the spices and the perfumes, the rich fragrance of the dishes of food and sweetmeats, the fruits and dates, the bread ... and the wine. Sense, too, the air of the day or night; breathe it in. Is it hot or cold? Pungent or sweet?

Think, maybe, of a wedding you have attended recently, or perhaps, even, your own wedding, if you are married. What aspects of a wedding do you really find enjoyable and what aspects tend to be unpleasant as far as you are concerned?

How does Mary initially notice that the wine is failing? What special, and, perhaps, womanly, quality, is it about her that she notices what seems to have passed unnoticed by so many other people? The significant compassionate note about this miracle, or "sign", is that such a lack of wine at the wedding would have been remembered for the rest of that couple's life. The first duty of a Jewish household would be hospitality, and a wedding is a particularly holy sign of God's covenant of love with the Jewish people.

Hear the tone of voice in which Mary addresses her Son. Try to experience its significant quality. Listen attentively to Jesus' response. "Woman" is an honoured title in the Middle East. How do you think Mary felt as her Son spoke to her? In this case it is worth knowing that it has echoes, too, which reach back into the past and forward into the future. "Woman" is also, therefore, a generic title, one which honours women, now. It is the chosen mode for many of Jesus' personal revelations to the whole of humanity. Women are often chosen to be the recipients of the Good News for all of humankind, in this way. Whenever the word "Woman" is used in the Gospel of John, particularly, try substituting the word "Humanity" ... and see what it does for the sense of the phrase. Don't be surprised if the result is a very much deeper and more significant meaning than you have ever noticed before in the words of Jesus.

"Humanity, what do you want from me?" Hear him say those words to you. What do you really want from him, for yourself and your own loved ones? What do you want for all of humankind? Tell him now.

Then, if you can, join in the action of the servants. Hear his mother speak to you and then pick up your pitcher and begin the task of going to the well, cranking up the bucket, and gradually filling the large ceremonial jars which may have been recessed into the ground, so large were they. There might have been no other way to draw the water than by ladling it out of these containers. How long does this task take you? Does it remind you of anything else in your life that has taken a very long time? Sometimes it may even be helpful to go to a tap and begin to fill a large bucket or vase from a small container. Let the water run over your hands and between your fingers. Actually experience the quality of the water. See its clarity. Perhaps you will even refresh your thirst with some. Gradually fill the vessel. Allow God to fill you in this way. Let God fill all the aspects of your life at the same time and allow yourself to become more and more full of God. This water can be you, too. You can be changed into the wine of deep joy and celebration in the knowledge that God fills and transforms you.

Now look at the warm colour of the water as it becomes wine. Enjoy its richness. Smell and savour it. Let it roll around your palate and feel its warmth as it now fills you. What is this mysterious quality of God that fills your senses? In what aspects of your life do you need to let God permeate you like this? Try now to hand over to God that area of your life. A gesture might help you at this point. You may find yourself speaking to Mary or to Jesus. If you do find this, don't be afraid to tell them anything that comes into your heart; the concerns of your family, the world, your day, your job prospects, your illness, or whatever. Or you may find yourself simply resting in the presence of God with no words. Well, just stay there gently, at home in the presence and love of God.

This is a rediscovery of God, the homemaker. Julian of Norwich has a wonderful phrase in which she describes God as "the astonishing familiarity of home". In the context of the beginnings of a new home, Jesus performs a sign which reveals his glory and an aspect of the reality of God. It is a sign of joy, hope, refreshment, warmth, colour and happiness in the beginnings of the home-life of a couple whose plight is noticed by his own mother.

Maybe you feel worried that this first wedding story features the "Virgin daughter of Israel", a title much loved for Hebrew women of significance, but in the next story we shall see that the message of Jesus is also for outsiders and foreigners. We meet a woman who in many ways represents some of the harder aspects of modern existence – the five-times-married Samaritan woman.

A Meeting at a Well

The Samaritan Woman

On the way he came to the Samaritan town called Sychar, near the land that Jacob gave to his son Joseph. Jacob's well is there and Jesus, tired by the journey, sat straight down by the well. It was about the sixth hour. When a Samaritan woman came to draw water, Jesus said to her, "Give me a drink". His disciples had gone into the town to buy food. The Samaritan woman said to him, "What? You are a Jew and you ask me, a Samaritan, for a drink?" – Jews, in fact, do not associate with Samaritans. Jesus replied:

"If you only knew what God is offering and who it is that is saying to you: Give me a drink, you would have been the one to ask, and he would have given you living water."

"You have no bucket, sir," she answered "and the well is deep: how could you get this living water? Are you a greater man than our father Jacob who gave us this well and drank from it himself with his sons and his cattle?" Jesus replied:

"Whoever drinks this water will get thirsty again; but anyone who drinks the water that I shall give will never be thirsty again: the water that I shall give will turn into a spring inside him, welling up to eternal life."

"Sir," said the woman "give me some of that water, so that I may never get thirsty and never have to come here again to draw water." "Go and call your husband" said Jesus to her "and come back here." The woman answered, "I have no husband". He said to her, "You are right to say, 'I have no husband'; for although you have had five, the one you have now is not your husband. You spoke the truth there." "I see you are a prophet, sir" said the woman. "Our fathers worshipped on this mountain, while you say that Jerusalem is the place where one ought to worship." Jesus said:

"Believe me, woman, the hour is coming when you will worship the Father neither on this mountain nor in Jerusalem. You worship what you do not know; we worship what we do know; for salvation comes from the Jews. But the hour will come – in fact it is here already – when true worshippers will worship the Father in spirit and truth: that is the kind of worshipper the Father wants. God is spirit, and those who worship must worship in spirit and truth."

The woman said to him, "I know that Messiah – that is, Christ – is coming; and when he comes he will tell us everything". "I who am speaking to you," said Jesus, "I am he."

At this point his disciples returned, and were surprised to find him speaking to a woman, though none of them asked, "What do you want from her?" or, "Why are you talking to her?" The woman put down her water jar and hurried back to the town to tell the people, "Come and see a man who has told me everything I ever did; I wonder if he is the Christ?" This brought people out of the town and they started walking towards him.

Many Samaritans of that town had believed in him on the strength of the woman's testimony when she said, "He told me all I have ever done", so, when the Samaritans came up to him, they begged him to stay with them. He stayed for two days, and when he spoke to them many more came to believe; and they said to the woman, "Now we no longer believe because of what you told us; we have heard him ourselves and we know that he really is the saviour of the world".

(John 4:5-30, 39-42)

W e have moved on to a very different scene from our first one. And yet one which evokes the previous encounter, in some ways.

In the wedding party story, Jesus chooses a young couple on which to focus his first great sign. His mother, too, is depicted as the Bride of God, who understands the divine destiny of her Son. Now, Jesus meets a woman from a despised minority group – the Samaritans. He meets her around water, once again; this time at a well. The location of a well would have reminded Christian-Jewish readers that their founding ancestors often met their predestined brides at a well. Isaac met Rebecca there and Jacob/Israel met his bride, Rachel, at a well. Because the well provided water in a desert country, it was taken to symbolise the gift of life from God to his people, embodied in a true marriage of loving persons who, together, would build up the people of God. However, in this dialogue, Jesus offers the gift of life to the most unlikely person we and his disciples can imagine.

Let's begin by visualising him as he approaches the well. The Gospel tells us that he was tired from his journey.

Feel, if you will, the weariness and tiredness in his body. Relate it, if you can, to times when you have experienced such tiredness, yourself. Maybe you have nursed a sick child or an ageing parent. Maybe you are actually experiencing such tiredness now, at this moment. Perhaps it is only life and its hectic pace that make you tired. Whatever it is, notice that Jesus feels tired, too, in the body that will later be our chief enduring memory of him and the way in which he remains present to us. Try to feel his thirst. Can you recall a time when you have been really thirsty? Perhaps you were ill and longing for a drink. Perhaps you have seen someone who was really thirsty. Can you relate your thirst to your life-situation? Maybe you will realise God's thirst, and, in some sense, God's need, for you, too. Notice that Jesus also feels frustration at not being able to draw a drink for himself.

Watch as Jesus settles himself by the well, and see the well itself, formed by the infiltration of many underground streams, gathering in one place. Try to still yourself down and listen to those tiny streams in a desert land gradually welling up into a source of water whose depths cannot be plumbed. Watch the creatures, some of them tiny and some of them large, which creep out in the darkness across the desert-floor to drink from those streams. Or, maybe, walk towards the well and gaze into its depths. Allow yourself to be swallowed up in its depth, which is the depth of God's own self. Try to see to the bottom. Look around you. Are there signs of green growth as so often is the case near a natural well, even one in a dry land? What other life does the well support apart from human life? Can you see the well's structure and what it is about it that prevents Jesus from reaching in and slaking his thirst?

In your imagination see the woman as she leaves the town of Sychar to draw water from the well which lies just outside the town. Notice her age, her carriage, her posture. She is alone. That is unusual, in itself, because women usually gathered together at the well to exchange greetings and gossip. If you can, then, see what goes on in this woman's heart. Notice, too, the person of Jesus as the woman approaches. What is it about her that draws Jesus to her and induces him to ask her to draw him up some water?

Notice the time of day – midday – the sixth hour. Feel the intense heat of the sun at noon in the Middle East. Is there any shade? If so, take yourself into the shade and watch what happens.

Try to see the expression on the woman's face as she approaches, and Jesus asks for a drink. See, too, their facial expressions change as the dialogue gets under way. Notice, particularly, the look of Jesus at the woman.

Hear the tone of his voice and the nature of her reply. Can you detect any humour? This is another one-to-one dialogue. The woman finds herself in a privileged relationship to Jesus where she is received positively and intimately. Perhaps you can imagine yourself in the same relationship with Jesus, either the historical Jesus or the Christ.

Join in the action. The conversion of Samaria relied on the belief of one (unlikely) woman disciple. Allow yourself to be that woman to whom Jesus reveals himself as "I am" and the "Water of Life". Allow Jesus to be that central revelation of God's action in you – of quite simply "being" who you are. Listen to who you might "become", so much so, that you, too, put down your water jar, immediately, as it were, and hasten away to follow Jesus, leaving whatever is *your* water jar in order to follow him.

Another way might be simply to *drink in* the "Water of Life" that is Jesus. Taste the freshness and clarity of God's presence in you.

This call of an unusual woman disciple is a call to recognise that God's powerful action can take effect in the way we least expect and through those persons we least expect to manifest it. The cultural unlikelihood of this Samaritan woman being called to discipleship was so great that John underlines it by describing the shock and surprise of Jesus' male disciples. We are made more aware of this because their shock is silent and they hardly dare express it.

Try to speak to Jesus directly, maybe pondering on the words of one of the other Samaritans:

"Now I believe, no longer because of what she told me; I have heard you myself and I know that you are, indeed, the Saviour of the World."

The
Light of Life

The Adulterous Woman

At daybreak he appeared in the Temple again; and as all the people came to him, he sat down and began to teach them.

The scribes and Pharisees brought a woman along who had been caught committing adultery; and making her stand there in full view of everybody, they said to Jesus, "Master, this woman was caught in the very act of committing adultery, and Moses has ordered us in the Law to condemn women like this to death by stoning. What have you to say?" They asked him this as a test, looking for something to use against him. But Jesus bent down and started writing on the ground with his finger. As they persisted with their question, he looked up and said, "If there is one of you who has not sinned, let him be the first to throw a stone at her". Then he bent down and wrote on the ground again. When they heard this they went away one by one, beginning with the eldest, until Jesus was left alone with the woman, who remained standing there. He looked up and said, "Woman, where are they? Has no one condemned you?" "No one, sir," she replied. "Neither do I condemn you," said Jesus "go away, and don't sin any more." When Jesus spoke to the people again, he said: "I am the light of the world."

(John 8:2-12)

This story is cleverly set in a frame of light – between daybreak in the Temple and Jesus' own statement about being the Light of the World, the Light of Life. Once again a woman will be the recipient of Jesus' revelation. On her life will the light of Christ be turned to illuminate the truth and to temper justice with mercy.

The story did not originally belong in John's Gospel, but it has been placed there by an early editor of the Gospel. Perhaps this was to show an example where a woman (as opposed to a man, e.g. Lazarus) is saved from death – brought back to life in every sense of the word.

The scene opens with Jesus, sitting in the Temple. A group of scribes and Pharisees bring along a woman, caught in the act of committing adultery. The man – the other perpetrator of the act – does not seem to be present. It is interesting that in the Mosaic law, only the man in a partnership could be sinned against. The sin lay in taking another man's wife rather than in betraying one's own wife. That the woman was caught in the act of adultery means that the couple were certainly observed together and the identity of the man must have been equally well known to the group. The betrayed husband probably had them observed closely.

Spend a moment with Jesus alone at daybreak – quieten yourself down and watch, with him, the daily miracle of sunrise. Be still, and drink in the colours of that particular moment on that particular day. Stay with him as long as you can, and then watch the people gather round him.

See the isolation of the woman as she is thrust forward to the centre of the group. Look around at the faces you can see. What can you detect in their eyes? Contempt? Hypocrisy?

What can you see in her eyes? Is fear a large part of her expression? Stoning was still practised here and there in Jewish society, at that time. It was seen as a way for the group to extract capital punishment for a crime without needing an executioner and thus, perhaps, violating the fifth commandment, "Thou shalt not kill."

Try to feel what the unknown woman must have been feeling at this time. It says, "they made her stand there in the middle, while they accused her", cleverly invoking Moses' instructions and putting Jesus to the test. Jesus was also being scrutinised. The group were trying to confront him with a choice between the law of Moses and the Roman law. What do you think Jesus, himself, was feeling at that moment? What do you imagine might have been his interior reaction to that question?

Now listen to the breathing of this unknown woman and be aware of the silence as Jesus ignores the question and begins to write with his finger on the ground. Why do you think he delayed? And what effect do you think the gesture had on the accusers and the bystanders? Try to put yourself in the place of the woman and experience what she was feeling at that time – and even now.

Listen, too, to the clamour and insistence of the group as they continue to put their question and press Jesus to an answer.

Watch Jesus as he bends down and begins to write in the sand. In the privacy of your prayer, it might be helpful to have a small tray of sand or dust and run your finger through it. Write something of significance to yourself. Freely make patterns, perhaps, but, whatever you do, associate yourself with the action of Jesus and open yourself consciously to any insight you may gain from his gesture. Such an activity can sometimes release feelings and insights we may otherwise miss.

When Jesus straightens up, try to notice the expression in his eyes and the tone with which he speaks those significant words. Has his expression or tone of voice changed? "If anyone is without sin, let the guiltless one be the first to throw a stone at her." What do those words mean to you?

Listen as the stones are discarded and the footsteps gradually recede. What heavy weights would you like to discard, yourself? Allow your own stones to drop from your hands, as Jesus looks at you, but stay around to watch his final encounter with the woman.

Watch him straighten up again – they are alone. Saint Augustine said of them, "Only they remain – Misery and Mercy" – the woman in her miserable condition, and Jesus, the merciful one. Watch the encounter between Misery and Mercy. You may also find yourself exploring all the areas of misery in our world today – war, famine, injustice. Place them before Christ as we ask how we, too, can practise mercy towards one another. Perhaps you will stand before Jesus in your own misery and experience the merciful love of God as Jesus speaks those words to you, to her.

> *"Neither do I condemn you,*
> *go away and sin no more."*

A Family Bereaved

The Resurrection Story about Martha, Mary and Lazarus

There was a man named Lazarus who lived in the village of Bethany with the two sisters, Mary and Martha, and he was ill. It was the same Mary, the sister of the sick man Lazarus, who anointed the Lord with ointment and wiped his feet with her hair. The sisters sent this message to Jesus, "Lord, the man you love is ill". On receiving the message, Jesus said, "This sickness will end not in death but in God's glory, and through it the Son of God will be glorified". Jesus loved Martha and her sister and Lazarus.

On arriving, Jesus found that Lazarus had been in the tomb for four days already. Bethany is only about two miles from Jerusalem, and many Jews had come to Martha and Mary to sympathise with them over their brother. When Martha heard that Jesus had come she went to meet him. Mary remained sitting in the house.

Martha said to Jesus, "If you had been here, my brother would not have died, but I know that, even now, whatever you ask of God, he will grant you". "Your brother" said Jesus to her "will rise again." Martha said, "I know he will rise again at the resurrection on the last day". Jesus said:

"I am the resurrection. If anyone believes in me, even though he dies he will live, and whoever lives and believes in me will never die. Do you believe this?"

"Yes, Lord", she said "I believe that you are the Christ, the Son of God, the one who was to come into this world." When she had said this she went and called her sister Mary, saying in a low voice, "The Master is here and wants to see you". Hearing this, Mary got up quickly and went to him. Jesus had not yet come into the village; he was still at the place where Martha had met him. When the Jews who were in the house sympathising with Mary saw her get up so quickly and go out, they followed her, thinking that she was going to the tomb to weep there.

Mary went to Jesus, and as soon as she saw him she threw herself at his feet, saying, "Lord, if you had been here, my brother would not have died". At the sight of her tears, and those of the Jews who followed her, Jesus said in great distress, with a sigh that came straight from the heart, "Where have you put him?" They said, "Lord, come and see". Jesus wept; and the Jews said, "See how much he loved him!" But there were some *who remarked, "He opened the eyes of the blind man, could he not have prevented this man's death?" Still sighing, Jesus reached the tomb; it was a cave with a stone to close the opening. Jesus said, "Take the stone away". Martha said to him, "Lord, by now he will smell; this is the fourth day". Jesus replied, "Have I not told you that if you believe you will see the glory of God?" So they took away the stone. Then Jesus lifted up his eyes and said:*

"Father, I thank you for hearing my prayer. I knew indeed that you always hear me, but I speak for the sake of all these who stand round me, so that they may believe it was you who sent me."

When he had said this, he cried in a loud voice, "Lazarus, here! Come out!" The dead man came out, his feet and hands bound with bands of stuff and a cloth round his face. Jesus said to them, "Unbind him, let him go free". (John 11:1-5, 17-44)

In this story Jesus brings new life and reunion to a family he loved dearly and visited on more than one occasion. Just as the last story was set in a frame of light, this story is set in a frame of love. It is unique in that the Gospel writer describes the closeness of the relationship, "Jesus loved Martha and her sister and Lazarus" ... and, later on, "See how much he loved him!" *(John 11:36).* The two sisters are the only women named in the Gospels as the object of Jesus' love. Lazarus, too, is the only man thus mentioned by name. This would seem to imply that these women, and Lazarus, were prominent among Jesus' disciples. In this account, a woman is the recipient of one of Jesus' most direct statements about himself and that same woman makes a heartfelt and accurate response to Jesus' words. There can be no doubt that women are equally drawn to the insights of faith and can equally respond as full disciples.

Lazarus is the object and Jesus the subject of this story, but it also closely involves the two women who play a more prominent part than their brother, even though Jesus raises him from the dead. It is especially Martha's faith that is scrutinised in this story. Both women are shown as being in the process of becoming true disciples of Jesus; to them, and especially to Martha, he reveals that he is the Resurrection and the Life.

You may wish to begin the story at verse 17 after Jesus has made the decision to return to the town of Bethany. In your imagination try walking that road with Jesus and his disciples. Picture to yourself the outskirts of the town and the locality.

Look around you, what can you see? What time of day is it? As you approach, what can you hear?

You may wish to visualise what Jesus sees as Martha makes her way out to meet him. She seems to be the elder sister and the householder – we can guess this because her name is always mentioned first in stories about the family (*cf. Luke 10*). She is clearly outgoing, probably an extrovert, and she it is who goes to meet Jesus first. She is very outspoken, but later we shall see that she is no less attached to Jesus than her sister, Mary, who comes across as much quieter. Try to enter into the feelings Martha is experiencing as she grieves for her brother. In what tone of voice do you hear her address Jesus: "Lord, if you had been here my brother would not have died?" What do you think Jesus, himself, was feeling as he heard her? You may have experienced bereavement yourself, and maybe you can recall the multiplicity of feelings you had when someone very close to you died? What was your overwhelming perception at the time, and how do you see that reality now? Martha can also represent anyone who has been left behind, and whose faith is challenged when a loved one dies. The dialogue between Jesus and Martha centres around this challenge to faith.

Maybe you feel bereaved in a way that has nothing to do with physical death. When Jesus responds, "I am the Resurrection and the Life", what do you understand by those words, if you relate them to your present life-situation? Grief and death can also be experienced in ways that affect the whole of society: global issues like war, famine, and exploitation of all kinds.

Jesus challenges Martha that he is the Resurrection and the Life, and that the eternal life he gives does not abolish death but transcends it. Jesus asks Martha, "Do you believe this?" Hear him ask that question of you and respond as openly as you can to an understanding of it and an acceptance of that possibility for faith. What areas of faith or belief in yourself and your own situation are challenged by Jesus in your prayer?

Martha's response to Jesus' question is less tentative than the Samaritan woman's response to him, for instance. Martha seems to understand that Jesus is, somehow, sent by God, but, as yet, she does not understand that Jesus is Life itself. However, her response is one of the clearest statements of belief in the Gospel and is equal to that of Peter. Try to find words like Martha's words to respond to Jesus. Tell him everything in your own heart. Borrow some of Martha's qualities and be candid in opening your heart to him.

Move on now, into the village, and see Mary's greeting of Jesus. She makes the same statement of loss and grief as Martha. She weeps so much that Jesus, too, is moved and greatly distressed. Sighing deeply, he asks to see where Lazarus is buried and begins to weep openly. Try to imagine the tears and sighs of Jesus. Some of the bystanders seem to be moved because they exclaim, "See how much he loved him." Listen to those tears and sighs with inner ears; watch Jesus with your inner eyes and respond as you feel called to do. Or else, just remain quiet and watchful.

Now imagine the place of the tomb. See the cave with the stone to close the opening. Reach out and touch the stone. Feel how unyielding it is. Now reach within yourself and touch anything that feels like stone, hard or unyielding, that is present in your life at the moment. Ask Jesus to touch the hardness as he was able to reach out and touch death, as he drew Lazarus back from the grave. "Take the stone away," he says. Notice that Martha is shocked. "By now he will smell," she says. Is there anything you would fear should Jesus dispel the hardness in you, just now? There is no need to be afraid. Jesus says to the women, "If you believe, you will see the glory of God." Try to open yourself to God, so that Jesus is able to touch the unyielding part of you and to move it away, calling forth the "you" that is full of life. Hear his voice call you forth as Lazarus was called forth. In the Eastern Church, many beautiful icons have been painted to show "The Raising of Lazarus". They often include a large group of people standing in the darkness of the cave alongside Lazarus. This is to remind us that we all need to be called forth from darkness and death into the life that is Christ. Realise that you don't have to come forth by your own efforts; Lazarus was called forth by the perfect prayer of Jesus. Hear in your heart those words of Jesus which give you complete freedom and life.

"Unbind her, let her go free."
"Unbind him, let him go free."

A
Gesture
of Love

Mary of Bethany
Anoints the Feet of Jesus

Six days before the Passover, Jesus went to Bethany, where Lazarus was, whom he had raised from the dead. They gave a dinner for him there; Martha waited on them and Lazarus was among those at table. Mary brought in a pound of very costly ointment, pure nard, and with it anointed the feet of Jesus, wiping them with her hair; the house was full of the scent of the ointment. Then Judas Iscariot – one of his disciples, the man who was to betray him – said, "Why wasn't this ointment sold for three hundred denarii, and the money given to the poor?" He said this, not because he cared about the poor, but because he was a thief; he was in charge of the common fund and used to help himself to the contributions. So Jesus said, "Leave her alone; she had to keep this scent for the day of my burial. You have the poor with you always, you will not always have me." (John 12:1-8)

This story describes an act of extravagant love and gratitude on the part of one of Jesus' women-disciples. It appears to rest strongly on a tradition that also appears in the Gospels of Mark and Matthew, and seems to have been, from earliest times, an important essential ingredient in understanding the Gospel message of Jesus, and the centrality Mary of Bethany held as a model of discipleship for the earliest Church. Mary is the only woman in the Gospels who is twice defended by Jesus for her choices. Her devotion to Jesus, and her desire to learn from him, are upheld by Jesus to her own sister, Martha. In this instance, Jesus defends her action to Judas and some of the other disciples. If, in the previous story, we were invited to reflect on Martha's faith, in this story we are presented with the example of Mary's devotion. Faith and devotion seem to go together. Perhaps Mary can model, for us, a way to deepen our personal attachment to the person of Jesus, as she surely did for the earliest Church.

The scene we are invited to contemplate is another Last Supper at which Jesus shares a meal with this particular family whom he loves. You may wish to make this a special prayer for your own family and its needs. A helpful way to enter into prayer might be to evoke the sort of atmosphere we have come to associate with the Last Supper: one in which Lazarus is present as the Beloved who represents all those restored by Jesus, while Mary performs an act of extravagant love which prefigures Jesus' own act of love demonstrated in the foot-washing of the Passover Supper. Jesus commends Mary for her love and associates her gesture with his Passion.

You might like to begin this time by trying to experience the feelings of Jesus, himself, as he gathers around him this group of a family and friends who are about to share a loving meal which they have prepared in Jesus' honour. It is only six days before the Passover and it does seem possible that Jesus may already have been experiencing some of the feelings that he had at his Last Supper – feelings of deep love and sadness at the same time. The most profound words and tenderest gestures are often kept for the moment of parting, and Mary seems to have had a premonition of this, which stemmed from her love of Jesus. Let us enter the room with her and watch the scene.

Look around you. What kind of room do you see? Who do you see present there, and what role do you have yourself? Try to pick up the atmosphere that is around and notice the main characters: Martha, Mary, Lazarus, Judas and, of course, Jesus. Particularly notice Lazarus, reclining at table with Jesus. What do you think are his feelings and what sort of conversation passes between Jesus and himself?

We are told that Martha is serving at table. What sort of woman do you see, and what do you imagine are her feelings as she offers food and drink to Jesus and his companions? It must have been a very intimate meal for Martha to wait on Jesus again. Usually, Jewish women only waited at table in the privacy of their own homes, so her act of service may have an even deeper meaning which you can, perhaps, discover by remaining with her for a while. Try to enter into her dispositions as you serve alongside her, offering this or that, clearing things away, maybe, and watching the glances and gestures with which Jesus responds to her and to you.

However, the main character of this story is Mary. Try to visualise her. What kind of woman is this who takes about a pint of the purest and most beautiful perfume and pours it on the feet of Jesus? Is she young or older – how do you see her? What do you think is happening within her as she decides to make this gesture? Do you think it was planned or done on impulse? What does the perfume mean to her and how does she come to have it in her possession? At what point in the meal does the gesture take place?

Notice that it doesn't matter how you visualise all of this but your own imagination will give you clues as to how you function in your relationships with God and with other people.

Now see Mary break the seal of the perfume jar and watch as she pours out the perfume. You can breathe in the fragrance which the Gospel writer tells us fills the entire house where the meal takes place. Try to imagine what Jesus feels as the perfume is poured on his feet and massaged into them. Now Mary unbinds her hair. This gesture alone is startling and a little scandalous. Only in private did Jewish women unbind their hair and Judas' anger may well have related as much to this gesture as to the cost of the ointment. See the tresses of Mary's hair as they tumble down and feel the quality of that hair as it mops up the perfume from the feet of Jesus. Wait for a moment and allow the perfume fully to pervade your senses. Be aware of it clinging to your own garments and filling your lungs, drawing you into its deepest meaning. What does this perfume signify for you?

Now imagine it reaching the nostrils of Judas. Why does he react with such anger? Do you identify with any of his anger? Imagine Jesus, later sensing the perfume on his own garments and, even, on his body, which is our chief enduring memory of him. What feelings and emotions might he be experiencing? Do you identify with any of those? What does the very action of "pouring out" bring to your mind? Is there any way now that you can offer all of this to God in prayer?

Hear, now, the conversation between Jesus and Judas – the objection of Judas and Jesus' reply, "Leave her alone; let her keep it for the day of my burial!" Have you ever felt yourself to be in a situation where you needed someone to defend you? Maybe this story can help you when you feel reproached by others for your choices and actions. More importantly, perhaps you can "catch", as it were, some of the loving devotion of Mary for the person of Jesus.

In the Gospel of Mark (*14:3-9)*, this story is also told with some variations. You may like to read that account, too, and hear the stirring words with which Jesus commends this courageous woman: "In truth I tell you; wherever throughout all the world the gospel is proclaimed, what she has done will be told as well, in remembrance of her."

Jesus wanted the action of that woman to be remembered. He must have valued her devotion very highly. As you close your prayer, you may wish to talk to Jesus and ask him for a deeper understanding of how highly he values you, too, and how you are imprinted on his memory for all time to come.

Twice, Jesus asks us to remember: firstly to remember this gesture, and, then, at the Last Supper, to remember him in the bread and wine which is his body and which Mary anoints in preparation for his death and burial.

The faithful disciple who is associated with the death of Jesus is also one who will experience the reality and power of his Resurrection.

Place
me with
your Son

A Woman Participating
in the "Hour" of Jesus

Near the cross of Jesus stood his mother and his mother's sister, Mary the wife of Clopas, and Mary of Magdala. Seeing his mother and the disciple he loved standing near her, Jesus said to his mother, "Woman, this is your son". Then to the disciple he said, "This is your mother". And from that moment the disciple made a place for her in his home.

After this, Jesus knew that everything had now been completed, and to fulfil the scripture perfectly he said:

"I am thirsty".

A jar full of vinegar stood there, so putting a sponge soaked in the vinegar on a hyssop stick they held it up to his mouth. After Jesus had taken the vinegar he said, "It is accomplished"; and bowing his head he gave up his spirit.

After this, Joseph of Arimathaea, who was a disciple of Jesus – though a secret one because he was afraid of the Jews – asked Pilate to let him remove the body of Jesus. Pilate gave permission, so they came and took it away. Nicodemus came as well – the same one who had first come to Jesus at night-time – and he brought a mixture of myrrh and aloes, weighing about a hundred pounds. They took the body of Jesus and wrapped it with the spices in linen cloths, following the Jewish burial custom. At the place where he had been crucified there was a garden, and in this garden a new tomb in which no one had yet been buried. Since it was the Jewish Day of Preparation and the tomb was near at hand, they laid Jesus there. (John 19:25-30, 38-42)

I n this passage the Gospel writer draws attention to a group of women who are disciples of Jesus. Once again the mother of Jesus steps from among them into sharper focus at the "hour" when it must have been the most harrowing moment of her life. Once again Mary is put forward as the image of the perfect disciple. At the foot of the cross of Jesus stand two people who will model, for us, perfect discipleship: a woman and a man, Mary and the Beloved Disciple. They will enact a drama which will take place at the very moment when Jesus surrenders his spirit to God in what he called his "Hour". As you move into the prayer, make this moment your "hour" with Jesus, whether it be a very short time, in actual fact, or a longer time that you have set apart.

This "hour" is the only other time, apart from Cana, that the mother of Jesus appears in the Gospel of John. In each of these two episodes, Jesus addresses her as "Woman". Once again she has a representational role for his disciples. Try changing the word to "Humanity" and you will easily see that you are meant to be included in the action. Mary's role becomes clear in the context of the "Hour" of Jesus, when Jesus hands over his life-spirit to those who are his disciples. Mary and the Beloved Disciple symbolise the larger group of disciples who will eventually be known as "Church". Mary becomes the mother, not only of the Beloved Disciple, but also of all those who through his death become the heirs of Jesus: his brothers and sisters in the Spirit. She symbolises a new relationship which will bind the Church and the Christian.

Now imagine the scene: the heat of the afternoon sun in the Middle East after a night and day characterised by injustice and violence. How might Mary be expected to feel? The burning sun, apart from anything else, would have caused the death of anyone exposed to it for very long. Mary, those other women, and the Beloved Disciple have stood for three hours watching and staying near to Jesus as he endured this wickedly ingenious way to cause maximum torment.

Try to enter the sorrowful scene at the foot of Jesus' cross and soak in the atmosphere: the anguish of those who are watching and their sheer inability to do something about the events. Maybe you will call to mind your own helplessness in the face of suffering or you will be reminded of the pointless suffering of many throughout our world today. If so, just remain silently in the presence of Jesus.

Maybe you are invited to step into the scene yourself. If so, look around you and try to see who else may be there. Watch the face of Jesus closely, as you would a loved one whose life is ebbing away. Apply your inner hearing to all the nuances of what he is saying to his mother and to the Beloved Disciple. Listen to his words as he commends his mother to the disciple's keeping. What expression do you see in his eyes as he looks at his mother? Hear his voice as he leaves us another gift – his own mother to be the mother of his followers.

It is in standing by Jesus in his darkest hour that Mary completes her relationship with Jesus. Stand, too, beside her, beside him. Ask God to place you with Jesus, the Son of God. Just remain in that place which elsewhere in his Gospel John describes as "nearest to the Father's heart" *(John 1:18)*.

Apply all your interior senses to the dispositions of Mary's heart which was already with Jesus in that place closest to the heart of God. Hear its silence, over against the clamour of the bystanders and the soldiers. See and experience the clarity of her heart in contrast to the darkness of this day and hour. Feel the softness and limpidity of her dispositions in contrast to the hardness of those bystanders. Reach and touch her, and permit her to touch you.

There is an ancient tradition that the body of Jesus was later placed in the arms of Mary when it was removed from the cross. Many artists have captured this poignant moment when Mary and the other women and men who were present grieve for their deep loss. You may have a favourite painting which may help you to enter this scene. More likely, you have probably sat by the bedside of a dying relative or friend. You can probably recall the effects of death and your own extreme helplessness in the face of events beyond your control. Maybe you feel able to experience the sheer weight of that beloved body. It may possibly remind you of weights, almost too heavy to bear, either in your own life or in the lives of others. Maybe you are a person who uses a global perspective in your prayer. Then, the weight may become the suffering of nations or the destruction of whole peoples. You may care to speak to Mary to help you to understand this weight.

When someone has been bereaved, there is an indefinable sense of waiting which many in our Western culture experience between death and final committal, whether by burial or cremation. This sense of waiting can take on an aspect of exquisite suffering and is not necessarily associated only with the bereavement we think of as death. You may have experienced this suffering with the breakdown of a marriage or the lack of communication between yourself and a teenager in the family, for example. Forced redundancy or the anxiety of debts can also provoke this feeling.

You may wish to speak with Mary or with Jesus, as you apply your prayer to yourself and your life. You may find yourself closing your prayer by thanking God for placing you so close to the Son. Or you may simply remain in silence as you contemplate this moment.

A Woman Proclaims the Resurrection

Mary Magdalen

It was very early on the first day of the week and still dark when Mary of Magdala came to the tomb. She saw that the stone had been moved away from the tomb and came running to Simon Peter and the other disciple, the one Jesus loved. "They have taken the Lord out of the tomb" she said "and we don't know where they have put him."

Meanwhile Mary stayed outside near the tomb, weeping. Then, still weeping, she stooped to look inside, and saw two angels in white sitting where the body of Jesus had been, one at the head, the other at the feet. They said, "Woman, why are you weeping?" "They have taken my Lord away" she replied "and I don't know where they have put him." As she said this she turned round and saw Jesus standing there, though she did not recognise him. Jesus said, "Woman, why are you weeping? Who are you looking for?" Supposing him to be the gardener, she said, "Sir, if you have taken him away, tell me where you have put him, and I will go and remove him." Jesus said, "Mary!" She knew him then and said to him in Hebrew, "Rabbuni!" – which means Master. Jesus said to her, "Do not cling to me, because I have not yet ascended to the Father. But go and find the brothers, and tell them: I am ascending to my Father and your Father, to my God and your God." So Mary of Magdala went and told the disciples, "I have seen the Lord", and that he had said these things to her.

(John 20:1-2, 11-18)

This is a New Creation story written around the personality of one of Jesus' most famous women-disciples. We know that it begins to retell the Creation story and, therefore, it re-aligns all our realities, giving them a freshness and clarity which have not been perceived before. We are conscious that the Gospel writer's opening words are intended to cast us back through time and evolution to the creative moment summarised in the book of Genesis. For those words, "It was very early and still dark", express the waiting and expectation of the cosmos before light and life are breathed into it. They call to mind the first day, when God separated Light from Darkness, with the words "Let there be Light." The earth was still a formless void in the shape of the tomb which Mary visits; darkness still hovered over the deep – it was "still dark" for Mary, too, and she was drawn back to the origins of life. A Man and a Woman will meet again at the dawn of God's Creation. What they bring to birth is the Church, a child of the Spirit who hovers over the waters. Jesus needed Mary to carry the message to all who recognise him and his Church. Therefore, she is able to say: "I have seen the Lord."

In spirit be with Mary on that first day. Experience the darkness with her. It may call to mind your own experience of grief, darkness or pain, when a single night seemed like a lifetime. Accompany this woman into the garden where the body of Jesus had been laid in a borrowed tomb. It is to a tomb that Mary hurries, evoking in our senses darkness, the stench of death, coldness and a lifeless silence. No doubt there will be instances in our own world which come to mind as you make this prayer. You may care to begin in this way, applying your senses to those realities and taking in the atmosphere.

Look around you, now. What kind of garden is this? Forget what you know about gardens in the Middle East and allow it to take shape in your mind. How do you enter the garden with Mary and with what moods and expectations are you filled? Listen to any sounds you can hear there.

Mary followed the two disciples back to the tomb after she had discovered that the body of Jesus had gone. But when the disciples had gone she stayed on, hoping against hope with the sort of tenacity all of us experience at times when we hang on against all reason.

What does that kind of hope actually feel like? The kind that has no foundation in rational behaviour – when we hang on, despite everything? She looks into the tomb, yet again, and, this time, she encounters angels.

Wait, now, with Mary outside the tomb. Stoop and look inside. Feel your body bend as you do so; bend your spirit, too, in anticipation. Allow the spirit of God to blow through your being, breathing into you life, breath, receptivity, in readiness for an encounter with your God. Try to prepare yourself with dispositions of "newness" or readiness to experience reality in a new way. Look once again into the tomb. What do you see? What, or who, are the angels? Try to perceive them in your mind's eye. Do they remind you of anything or anyone who has influenced your life in any way? Hear their question as though it were addressed to you. "Why are you weeping?" What do you answer them?

Move out into the garden, now, with Mary. Is it the same garden as the one you entered a short time ago? Or have the angels had any effect on you? What kind of effect do they seem to have had on Mary?

The drama heightens. Now Mary turns and is confronted by Jesus, himself. We know this; you even know it in your prayer, somehow, but Mary doesn't yet know that this is Jesus! Try to be with her as she meets the one she has loved so much. Maybe you are already thinking of moments in your own life when God was mysteriously present in persons or in circumstances and, maybe later, you somehow just knew that. What does that level of knowledge actually feel like?

Jesus greets Mary as "Woman". Once again that is the clue that something momentous is about to happen. Once again a woman is put in the position of representing all of humanity as Jesus singles her out for the greatest revelation, yet, about himself. Include yourself in the question, then, as Jesus prepares to reveal himself to you in his Risen Life. This woman was chosen to be the first to see and understand the Risen Jesus: be with her at this moment as he asks you, "Why are you weeping; humanity, who are you looking for?"

We noticed at the beginning of this book that all of Jesus' words to women and revelations of himself in John's Gospel take on the form of an intimate dialogue with the person who is the recipient of the Good News, for elsewhere in the same Gospel Jesus says, "I have called you friends, because I have made known to you everything I have learnt from my Father" *(John 15:15)*. Now, too, Jesus addresses Mary by the intimate form of her name, "Mariam", and she immediately recognises him. She cannot mistake his voice when he speaks to her personally.

"Do not be afraid: I have called you by your name; you are mine" *(Isaiah 43:1)*.

Allow Jesus, now, to call you by your own name. Say it to yourself, interiorly. Try to hear his voice saying your name with your inner hearing. Hear any nuances that are there and try to respond with a full heart as Mary responds, hearing the sound of a voice which she thought was gone for ever: "My Master!"

You may wish to do what Mary did: to grasp hold of Jesus, so great is your joy. Her one reaction seems to have been to rush forward and hold him. His prohibition surely stems from being overwhelmed by the exuberance of her greeting. If you could see his face at this moment, what do you think his expression would register? Allow yourself to experience his gracious touch. Reach out and touch him yourself, holding and being held in whatever way seems right and most appropriate to you. But notice, too, that Jesus is using this incident to emphasise that his permanent future presence to his disciples (and to you) is not necessarily by appearance, or by touch, but by way of the Spirit who will fill each of his followers. Maybe you have already experienced this new presence of God which is sometimes characterised by absence?

Listen to Jesus' words to Mary. He tells her to go and to find and then to tell. See if you can associate yourself with this commission. Maybe you even need to find and to tell yourself as you prepare yourself to receive the Holy Spirit.

For whatever reason, Jesus chose first to appear to his women-followers, and particularly to Mary Magdalen, who was given the unique experience of being the first to see the Risen Lord. By the time the Fourth Gospel came to be written the customary Easter proclamation and the hallmark of apostleship was the statement: "I have seen the Lord."

The Gospel writer puts these words on the lips of Mary in acknowledgement of the fact that she bears the first apostolic witness to the new and risen life with which Jesus endows his Church.

As you close your prayer, align yourself with her and notice moments in your life when you have been enlightened in some way so that you understood God's action in your life more fully, enabling you to say, with Mary Magdalen, "I have seen the Lord."

You may wish to close your prayer, then, by permitting yourself to feel the warmth of God's gracious love as you would experience the heat of the sun. Bask in God's goodness, then, as a sunbather basks – or you may care to lift your face to the refreshing stream of God's grace as a tired and weary traveller stands beneath a cascade of water, after a long and tiring journey. If you can do this – remain there in thanksgiving for the graces of your life.